D1404310

THE WRIGHT BROTHERS

By Gretchen Will Mayo

WORLD ALMANAC® LIBRARY

Please visit our web site at: www.worldalmanaclibrary.com
For a free color catalog describing World Almanac® Library's list
of high-quality books and multimedia programs, call 1-800-848-2928 (USA)
or 1-800-387-3178 (Canada). World Almanac® Library's fax: (414) 332-3567.

Library of Congress Cataloging-in-Publication Data

Mayo, Gretchen.
    The Wright brothers / by Gretchen Will Mayo.
      p. cm. — (Trailblazers of the modern world)
    Includes bibliographical references and index.
    Summary: A biography of the bicycle makers whose fascination with flight led them to build and fly
the world's first successful aircraft powered by an engine and controlled by a pilot.
    ISBN 0-8368-5094-7 (lib. bdg.)
    ISBN 0-8368-5254-0 (softcover)
    1. Wright, Orville, 1871-1948—Juvenile literature. 2. Wright, Wilbur, 1867-1912—Juvenile literature.
3. Aeronautics—United States—Biography—Juvenile literature. 4. Inventors—United States—Biography—
Juvenile literature. [1. Wright, Orville, 1871-1948. 2. Wright, Wilbur, 1867-1912. 3. Inventors.
4. Aeronautics—Biography.] I. Title. II. Series.
TL540.W7M379   2003
629.13'0092'273—dc21
[B]   2003042290

First published in 2004 by
World Almanac® Library
330 West Olive Street, Suite 100
Milwaukee, WI 53212 USA

Project manager: Jonny Brown
Editor: Jim Mezzanotte
Design and page production: Scott M. Krall
Photo research: Diane Laska-Swanke
Indexer: Walter Kronenberg

Photo credits: © Bettmann/CORBIS: 5, 6 bottom, 35, 36, 42 bottom, 43 top; © CORBIS: 38 bottom; Courtesy of
Special Collections and Archives, Wright State University: 8 both, 10 both, 14, 18, 21 top, 22, 23, 24, 25 top, 28, 29,
31 bottom, 37, 38 top, 39, 40; © Hulton Archive/Getty Images: 6 middle, 34; © Hulton-Deutsch Collection/CORBIS:
6 top; Scott M. Krall/© World Almanac® Library, 2004: 21 bottom, 25 bottom; © Lester Lefkowitz/CORBIS: 43
bottom; © Library of Congress: cover, 12, 16, 19, 26, 27, 30, 31 top, 42 top

Printed in the United States of America

1 2 3 4 5 6 7 8 9 07 06 05 04 03

TABLE of CONTENTS

Words that appear in the glossary are printed in **boldface** type the first time they occur in the text.

CHAPTER 1

THE FIRST BIRDMEN

On December 17, 1903, Orville and Wilbur Wright's flying machine lifted from the ground and flew 120 feet (37 meters)—less than the width of a football field. Orville was in the air for twelve seconds, but his short flight changed humankind forever. The Wright brothers had built and flown the world's first successful aircraft powered by an engine and controlled by a pilot.

TO FLY LIKE A BIRD!

The admiring French called the Wright brothers "the first birdmen." Long before their historic achievement, Orville and Wilbur Wright had watched soaring, swooping birds and wondered, how do they do it? The brothers were certainly not the first people to ask such a question—or to dream of flight. In 1678, for example, a French locksmith named Besnier strapped on artificial wings and attempted to fly from a high window. While the wings broke his fall, they did not keep him aloft like the neighborhood pigeons.

Even before Besnier, people made wings of wood and fabric and took their chances with a leap into the air. Their attempts at flight usually ended with spectacular, often deadly, crashes. Some people, however, had limited success—and lived to tell their tales.

In A.D. 875, a Muslim doctor in Spain named Abu'l-Kasim Abbas Firnas attached artificial wings with feathers to his body. He made the first successful glider flight, although he did seriously injure his back when landing.

In A.D. 1010, an English Benedictine monk named Eilmer risked his life to prove he could fly. Wearing wings made of linen stretched over a wooden frame and covered with feathers, he jumped from the top of an abbey tower and made a lucky glide. A fellow monk reported that Eilmer caught a breeze and sailed more than 660 feet (200 m). Unfortunately, he broke both legs when landing and walked with a limp the rest of his life.

Leonardo da Vinci, the brilliant Italian artist and scientist, studied birds in hopes of learning the secrets of flight. During the late 1400s, he filled notebooks with detailed sketches of birds' muscles and bones. Then, he drew designs for flying machines. But the great da Vinci's ideas never became reality.

This design for a flying machine was created in the early 1800s.

THE QUEST TO UNDERSTAND

Although Orville and Wilbur dreamed of flight, they were not daredevils. Instead of leaping from windows, the Wrights first studied the science of **aeronautics** and then began flight experiments with a kite.

In England, a man named Sir George Cayley had studied birds in flight to understand how their wings worked. The Wright brothers, who had also studied

Otto Lilienthal, *ca.* 1896

Octave Chanute, *ca.* 1896

A flying machine created by Dr. Samuel P. Langley

Pioneers in Experimental Flying

Otto Lilienthal, a German engineer, became famous for his gliding experiments. In the 1890s, he designed and built sixteen different versions of his unusual glider, which held him aloft on two or more curved, batlike wings. The Wright brothers admired Lilienthal's courage, and they also made note of his calculations.

In the United States, Octave Chanute, an engineer renowned for building the first bridge across the wide Missouri River, also became a gliding pioneer. Inspired by Otto Lilienthal's work, Chanute began building his own kind of glider. While Chanute gave directions, his younger associates made hundreds of test flights, taking off from the windswept dunes along the southern shore of Lake Michigan. Wilbur Wright eventually started a ten-year correspondence with Chanute.

Dr. Samuel Pierpont Langley, the respected head of the Smithsonian Institution in Washington, D.C., also conducted flight experiments. He spent ten years testing models of his airplanes, called aerodromes, before deciding which design held the greatest promise for a full-sized craft. In October 1896, Dr. Langley successfully launched two unmanned model aerodromes from the top of a houseboat in the Potomac River. The U.S. Army gave him $50,000 to continue his work, and the Smithsonian added $200,000. Dr. Langley was confident he could build a full-sized, powered flying machine that could be ridden and controlled in the air by a human, but his efforts were never successful.

birds, read Cayley's ideas and thought they made sense. Cayley noticed that, in flight, a bird's wings were curved, not flat, so he designed arched kites. He devoted much of his life to flight experiments and learned a lot about how wings create **lift**. In 1853, he built a glider that carried his protesting coachman a short distance in the air. (The coachman was so shaken that he quit on the spot.)

The Wright brothers also built gliders, which they flew many times. They learned firsthand that gliding was a risky activity, pitting the glider's fragile wings against the unpredictable forces of a churning sea of air. With no power, a glider was at the mercy of shifting currents and sudden **downdrafts**.

In the late 1800s, scientists studying flight believed that an engine-powered aircraft would be needed to truly fly in a controlled manner, and the Wright brothers agreed. Some of these powered machines had already been tested, and their crashes made headlines. But three pioneers in aeronautics were carrying out experiments that seemed to put them ahead of the crowd. From the brothers' hometown of Dayton, Ohio, they read with growing interest about the efforts of German engineer Otto Lilienthal and fellow Americans Octave Chanute and Samuel Pierpont Langley.

When these three men were conducting their aeronautical experiments, Orville and Wilbur Wright were newcomers to the exploration of flight. In Dayton, they were busy manufacturing bicycles. But they kept up with the work of the famous pioneers.

Wilbur noted that "men of the very highest standing in professions of science and invention had attempted to solve the problem" of controlled air flight. So far, none had succeeded.

Why did the bicycle makers of Dayton triumph, while all of the others failed? The answer begins with their youngest years.

CHAPTER 2

BORN ENGINEERS

Mechanical toys and gadgets fascinated Wilbur and Orville throughout life. As very small children, the boys tinkered with playthings, taking them apart and assembling them again. When toys broke, the boys learned from their mother how to repair them.

They seemed to have inherited their mother's mechanical ability. Susan Koerner Wright built many simple household appliances for herself. Family members said she could mend anything. Shy but devoted to her family, Susan made toys and built a sled for her children.

The brothers' father, the Reverend Milton Wright, passed on to Orville and Wilbur a lifelong confidence in their own abilities. Milton and Susan believed in strong family ties and self-education. They filled their home with books, encouraging their four sons and youngest child, Katharine, to read widely but think for themselves.

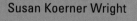

Susan Koerner Wright

Reverend Milton Wright

WILL AND ORV: DIFFERENT PERSONALITIES

Wilbur was the Wright's middle child. Born on April 16, 1867, near Millville, Indiana, he arrived well after brothers Reuchlin and Lorin and before Orville and Katharine. Will was a handsome, quiet boy who loved to read. He was an excellent student, especially in mathematics, but some teachers saw him as a daydreamer. Will was less likely to speak up in class than his little brother, Orville, who was often assigned a seat in the front row of the classroom under the watchful eye of his teacher.

Orville, born on Aug 19, 1871 in Dayton, Ohio, was fun-loving around family and friends but shy among strangers. Orv loved to tackle a challenge and quickly took to any new gadget. He always remembered his fifth birthday for the gyroscope his father gave him and the fun he had with it.

Thinking Together

Late in life, Wilbur wrote about the unusually close relationship he enjoyed with Orville.

"From the time we were little children my brother Orville and myself lived together, played together, worked together and, in fact, thought together. We usually owned all of our toys in common, talked over our thoughts and aspirations so that nearly everything that was done in our lives has been the result of conversations, suggestions and discussions between us."

PARENTS WHO INSPIRED THEIR CHILDREN

Orville was seven years old and Wilbur was eleven when their father was made Bishop of the Church of the United Brethren in Christ. The family moved often and Bishop Wright had to travel for months at a time to visit congregations. But frequent family letters kept him in close touch. He urged his children to be **enterprising** and earn their own pocket money. Susan paid Will and

Wilbur Wright, age 12

Orville Wright, age 8

Orv for making household repairs or gave each boy a penny for wiping dishes. The boys weren't scolded for spending their income on hobbies. Bishop Wright encouraged his children's curiosity and often returned home from church trips carrying toys or interesting books.

One day, the bishop gave his sons a toy that resembled a modern helicopter. With a toss, the toy fluttered near the ceiling before falling to the floor. The bishop explained that Alphonse Penaud, a Frenchman interested in aeronautics, had invented it. The boys named the new toy "the bat." Over the years, they built many copies. But as Orville remarked as an adult, "When we undertook to build the toy on a much larger scale it failed to work as well." The brothers had run into a problem that later affected their work with flying machines.

When Orville was eleven years old and searching for a way to earn money, he taught himself to build kites. He constructed a framework so light and thin that it bent with the wind. The kites flew unusually well, and he sold many of them. Years later, when studying aircraft design, Orville realized his kites had flown so well because the curved surface created lift.

WILBUR'S LOST HOPES

While Orville explored moneymaking schemes in his spare time, Wilbur was earning high marks in his high school classes. He showed a gift for writing, but he also starred in gymnastics. Wilbur hoped to attend Yale University.

In June 1884, Wilbur was only weeks away from his high school graduation in Richmond, Indiana, when Bishop Wright decided to move his family back to Dayton, Ohio. Instead of finishing his senior year in a new school, Wilbur took on the job of business manager for his father's church paper. Wilbur still planned to go to college, but an accident changed his life forever.

Wilbur was playing "shinny," an ice skating game similar to street hockey, when he was smashed in the mouth with a hockey stick. All of his front teeth were knocked out. During the long months of recovery, serious complications set in. Wilbur, who had always been handsome, athletic, and smart, was so sickly that he began to think the future he had planned was lost. He became deeply depressed.

At the same time, Susan Wright was growing desperately ill with **tuberculosis** and needed someone to care for her. Wilbur spent the next three years tied to the house, tenderly caring for his dying mother while educating himself in the family library.

FROM HOBBY TO BUSINESS

Orville, meanwhile, had discovered the craft of printing. From experiments with wood engraving when he was twelve, Orv progressed to operating a small printing press with an old friend, Ed Sines. To help the boys,

Out of the Scrap Pile

When Orv and Will were young, they frequenty used the scrap pile in creative ways. To make Orv's lathe run more smoothly, Will salvaged metal rings from an old harness and marbles to use as ball bearings. Later, with Will's help, Orv built his own printing press from a damaged tombstone, buggy parts, scrap metal, and odd junkyard objects.

Wilbur and Lorin traded an old boat for the press and the bishop donated twenty-five pounds of used type. But when the boys printed *The Midget*, a newspaper for their classmates, the Bishop censored it for the comments written about teachers.

Orville and Ed eventually started a printing business. Promising lower prices than any other printing house in town, they turned out handbills, tickets, business cards, envelopes, and stationery. Orville was so

The Wright family home on Hawthorn Street in Dayton, Ohio, *ca.* 1900

taken with printing that he worked as an **apprentice** at a local printing shop during summers and decided not to complete his senior year of high school so he could pursue the printing business.

Orville bought out Ed's share of the printing shop and hired him as an employee to run the presses, and he persuaded Wilbur to help him build a larger printing press out of scraps. Together, the brothers published the *West Side News*, a popular weekly community newspaper. The next year, they turned it into the daily *Evening Item*, with Wilbur editing. Competition from larger newspapers in the area eventually forced the brothers to shut down the newspaper. The brothers continued operating the printing shop, but they were ready for a fresh challenge.

A NEW HOBBY

Orv and Will had read about new-fangled "safety bicycles," which were first made in England. Before the safety bicycle, a rider sat atop a front wheel that was much taller than the rear wheel, and a fall could cause serious injury. With the safety, the rider sat between two small, equally sized wheels fitted with air-filled tires that could absorb bumps. This new design sparked a bicycle craze. In the spring of 1892, Orville caught the fever and splurged on a brand new Columbia model. A few weeks later, Wilbur bought a used version.

Although no one could have predicted it at the time, cycling on land would eventually lead the Wright brothers to their adventures in the air.

CHAPTER 3

FROM BIKES TO KITES

The Wright brothers soon came to love cycling. Wilbur enjoyed exploring country roads on long rides, while Orville was hooked on racing. Since they were also good mechanics, their friends asked for bicycle repairs. Before long, the brothers decided they should turn their new hobby into a business. In December of 1892, they opened a bicycle sales and repair shop next to their printing plant.

As the bicycle fever heated, other shops also opened. Will wondered if he and Orv should build their own bicycles. The brothers then turned the back room and second floor of Wright's Cycle into a light machine shop.

Unlike other bicycle makers, the Wright brothers refused to mass-produce their bicycles. Perfectionists at heart, they hand made each Wright Cycle with careful attention to details, even constructing tools for making bicycle parts. Orville loved improving on other manufacturers' bicycles. He also had a sense of humor. At one point, he and Will pedaled around in a gigantic bicycle-built-for-two, which they had made from four-foot tall front wheels salvaged from old-style bikes.

The brothers' bicycle and print shops turned a good profit, but by 1896 Will felt trapped. He was twenty-nine years old, exceptionally smart, yet he was still doing work that didn't challenge his problem-solving abilities.

The Wright brothers' cycle shop in Dayton, Ohio. The brothers built their first flying machine in the rear addition that can be seen behind the main brick building.

Then, in August of 1896, at the height of the success of Wright Cycle, Orville was struck down by deadly **typhoid fever**. He lay delirious throughout September. When his fever finally broke in October, Will shared disturbing news. Otto Lilienthal, the great German designer of gliders whom the brothers greatly admired, had died after breaking his back in a gliding accident. Wilbur and Orville had published an article about Lilienthal during their newspaper days. His death stirred up Wilbur's childhood questions about flight, as well as thoughts about Lilienthal's unfinished work.

WILBUR'S FIRST STEP INTO HISTORY

Still fascinated with the idea of human flight, Wilbur wrote to the Smithsonian Institution two years later requesting aeronautical information. "I wish to avail myself of all that is already known," he wrote. Wilbur also turned to flight pioneer Octave Chanute for further advice.

Studying everything he could find about the history of flying experiments, Wilbur brilliantly untangled three basic requirements for human flight. First, a successful heavier-than-air flying machine needed curved wings. Second, it would require some form of power to propel it through the air. Third, the machine had to be balanced and controllable or it would crash.

Today, these basic elements of flight seem laughably simple. For generations, however, experimenters had failed to seriously address the third requirement— control in the air. Even Langley and Chanute had decided they would deal with control after achieving flight. The Wrights were alone in understanding that flying an airplane successfully was impossible without control. Cycling had taught them that no one could stay on two wheels without making constant shifts and adjustments. To avoid crashing, wouldn't a pilot need the same kind of control over an airplane?

Problem Solvers

The Wright brothers have been described as high school dropouts who turned out to be geniuses. The truth is not so simple. Both brothers were extremely intelligent, and they were avid readers who educated themselves. But were they geniuses? Maybe not in the way that people often think of genius. Their brilliant solutions to the problems of flight did not come to them easily. They questioned and rethought as they read, and they had a knack for noticing connections between ideas that seemed unrelated at first glance. Like many inventors, they were good at imagining an object, turning it over in their minds, and forming new images of it. Most importantly, they insisted on solving all the problems of one phase of their work before going on to the next phase. With Wilbur's ability to envision each necessary goal and Orville's talent with details, the brothers had a winning combination.

Wilbur (left) and Orville test their first glider as a kite in 1899.

ONE STEP AT A TIME

The brothers were not about to take dangerous risks. They decided to fly a glider first so they could figure out how to make an airplane that a person could control. In July 1899, they began building a **biplane** kite. To control the kite, they rigged it with wires that could twist, or warp, the kite's wings. When Will tested the kite over a field near Dayton, he maneuvered it with such balanced swoops and dips that nearby boys dived to the ground.

The brothers built a biplane glider based on the design of the kite. It had a **wingspan** of 17 feet (5 m) and was able to carry a person on the bottom wing who could operate the wing-warping wires.

Wing-warping Magic

To steer during flight, gliding pioneers shifted the weight of their hanging legs, a method that resulted in Otto Lilienthal's death. Wilbur Wright's study of birds gave him clues to a better method. "The thought came to me that possibly [the bird] adjusted the tips of its wings," he wrote. Perhaps a bird balanced itself in air currents by positioning the edge of one wingtip up and the other down. But could rigid man-made wings be designed to act the same way?

The answer came one day in July 1899, when Wilbur was working in the bicycle shop. While absent-mindedly twisting an empty, rectangular box in his hands, he suddenly imagined the wings of a glider. Twisting, or warping, was the solution. Using control wires, a pilot could throw a spiral twist across an entire wingspan to bank or regain balance.

KITTY HAWK

When the glider was ready to be tested, the brothers searched for a spot with reliable winds of around 15 miles (24 km) per hour, an elevated launching spot, and bare, open country. No place near Dayton filled the bill, but by contacting the National Weather Bureau, they found a winner in Kitty Hawk, North Carolina.

The Wrights asked their friend, Charlie Taylor, to mind the cycle shop so they could leave town. William Tate, Kitty Hawk's postmaster, helped make arrangements and invited Wilbur to stay with his family while assembling the glider, which had been shipped in pieces.

Wilbur uses sand to clean a pan at the Wrights' Kitty Hawk camp in 1900.

Wilbur stepped onto Kitty Hawk's shore on September 13, 1900, after a trip involving two trains, a steamer, a small boat and a broken-down fishing schooner. He looked across the barren strip of sand. Only a scattering of houses, two lifesaving stations, a weather station, and a cluster of sand dunes called the Kill Devil Hills broke Kitty Hawk's broad, flat landscape.

When Orville arrived, the brothers pitched a tent on the sand, away from the settlement. Life out on the coastal strand was no picnic. The brothers had to carry their water over 1,000 feet (305 m) to their tent. For flight-testing, they dragged their glider 4 miles (6 kilometers) to the dunes and then 100 feet (161 m) up Big Kill Devil Hill. Despite these hardships, in October Orv wrote to sister Kate, "We have been having a fine time, altogether we have had the machine out three different days, from 2 to 4 hours each time."

Wilbur wrote to Octave Chanute. "I think at least a hundred buzzards, eagles, ospreys, and hawks made their home within a half mile of our camp." He explained that hours of watching birds in flight gave him solid answers to questions "which have been much disputed" among aeronautical scholars.

The brothers first flew the glider as a kite. Then, they began piloting the glider in short flights launched from Big Kill Devil Hill. A strong gust of wind eventually wrecked the glider, but not before Orv and Will had flown it successfully a dozen times.

They were ready to build a bigger and better glider for tests in 1901.

The 1900 glider was a success at Kitty Hawk, even though it was eventually wrecked by a gust of wind.

CHAPTER 4

PATIENCE AND DETERMINATION

In July 1901, with Charlie Taylor once again watching the cycle shop, the Wrights departed for Kitty Hawk. They had high hopes for their new glider. Its larger wingspan—22 feet (6.7 km)—required more lift, so the brothers had carefully followed calculations made by Otto Lilienthal when increasing the curve of the wings.

From the day the brothers arrived in mid-July, they were attacked by hordes of mosquitoes. Orville wrote Katharine that there was no escape. "They chewed us clear through our underwear and 'socks.' Lumps began swelling up all over my body like hen's eggs." Unpredictable winds and weather also plagued the Wrights.

As if these difficulties were not bad enough, the new glider performed badly. The changes made to increase lift had failed. Worse, the wing-warping system did not control the glider as the brothers had expected. In flight, the glider climbed upward rapidly or stalled and nosed down. Flying at Kitty Hawk had turned unpredictable and dangerous. "This is precisely the fix Lilienthal got into when he was killed," Orv wrote to Kate.

Although they had broken distance records piloting the largest glider ever flown, the brothers decided to pack up and return to Dayton early. On the train ride home, a despondent Wilbur told Orville. "Not within a thousand years will man ever fly!"

A DARING DECISION

Uncertainty always made Wilbur nervous. He and Orv had fully trusted the calculations for lift handed down by Chanute, Langley, and Lilienthal. Now, after reviewing their own measurements, the Wrights were forced to doubt everything.

In a daring move, the brothers decided to throw aside all calculations made by others and start from scratch. Spending the winter and spring in their bicycle workshop, they designed and built their own wind tunnel. The brothers made nearly two hundred small, model wing shapes, called **airfoils**, and used the wind tunnel to test the airfoils in different air conditions.

Their wind tunnel research was tedious and exacting. But the new information the Wrights gained marked a turning point in the history of aviation, and the brothers knew it. Each day was filled with the excitement of discovery. "Wilbur and I could hardly wait for morning to come to get at something that interested us. That's happiness!" Orville recalled later.

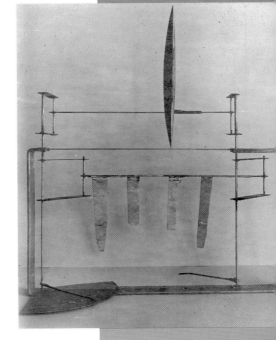

An airfoil, with the balance device below it, used to test wing shapes in the Wright brothers' wind tunnel

A wing's shape determines the amount of lift it can produce.

Groundbreaking Research

Many scientists have argued that the Wrights' most important contribution to aeronautics was the research they accomplished two years before their historic flight in 1903. The Wrights' wind tunnel was a box 6 feet (1.8 m) long with a fan at one end and a window for viewing on top. Inside the tunnel, a small, delicate device made from spokes and blades held an airfoil while the fan blew a steady stream of air at 27 miles (43 km) per hour.

For months the brothers experimented with little airfoils of different sizes and shapes. From this work, they were able to find the wing shapes that produced the most lift. Recording the data in their notebooks, they replaced old air-pressure tables with their own.

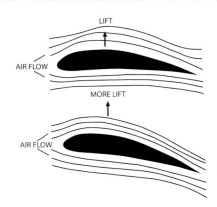

LIFT

AIR FLOW

MORE LIFT

AIR FLOW

THE REMARKABLE 1902 GLIDER

Working with their own new tables for air pressure, the Wrights confidently designed a larger biplane glider in 1902. It had a wingspan of 32 feet (9.8 m).

Writing to her father on August 20th, Katharine described her brothers' last minute preparations for their 1902 trip to Kitty Hawk. "The flying machine is in process of making now," she wrote. "Will spins the sewing machine around by the hour while Orv squats around marking places to sew. There is no place in the house to live."

The brothers made nearly a thousand glides at Kitty Hawk in 1902. They improved their operating skills and recorded their constant observations about flight problems. In about one glide in fifty, the machine lost balance mysteriously. Orville's idea to change the fixed tail into a moveable vertical **rudder**, and Wilbur's idea to connect the rudder wires to those for wing-warping, solved the problem.

At last, the Wrights' glider handled the Kitty Hawk winds reliably. The brothers had proven the accuracy of their calculations. They were ready to build a powered machine.

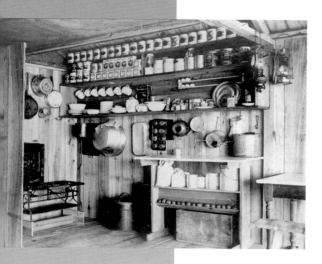

The neatly organized kitchen at the Kitty Hawk camp demonstrates Orville's attention to detail.

HORSEPOWER AND WHIRLING WINGS

Back in Dayton, Orv and Will searched for a gasoline engine that weighed less than 200 pounds (60 kilograms) and produced eight **horsepower**. When they could not find an existing engine to fit these requirements, they asked Charlie Taylor, a skilled mechanic, to help them

The Wrights' 1902 glider soars from Big Kill Devil Hill, with the brothers' camp visible in the distance. Although the 1902 glider made over 250 successful flights in two days, the U.S. patent office denied the brothers a patent for the machine, claiming it was incapable of flight.

Patent Problems

As Octave Chanute spoke to flight enthusiasts about the Wright's accomplishments, the brothers began to receive questioning letters about the design of their glider. Even the famous Samuel Langley wanted to watch the glider fly. Chanute worried that someone might steal the Wright's design ideas to beat them in the race to fly a powered machine. At Chanute's urging, Wilbur applied for a **patent** to protect his and Orville's inventions.

The Wrights and Chanute were shocked when the U.S. Patent Office insisted that the 1902 glider was not capable of flying and swiftly denied a patent. When Wilbur applied again, he received a second rejection without a hearing.

build one. In only six weeks, the three men designed and constructed an engine that generated at least twelve horsepower and weighed 179 pounds (81 kg).

Charles Taylor (third from right), stands with Wilbur Wright (second from right) and others in front of a Flyer in 1909. Taylor, a skilled machinist, was the Wrights' only employee for many years, and he helped build the 1903 Flyer.

Propellers were a bigger challenge, since little was known about them in 1902. Orville and Wilbur once again refused to make guesses. For months the brothers studied, experimented, and argued, filling more than five notebooks with information. "Our minds became so obsessed with it that we could do little other work," Orville wrote later. But through their process, the Wrights became the first to understand that a propeller works like a rotating wing. "Isn't it astonishing that all these secrets have been preserved for so many years just so that we could discover them!" Orville said.

Arguing Their Way To Answers

Charlie Taylor overheard many Wright discussions. "Both boys had tempers," Charlie remembered. "They would shout at one another something terrible. I don't think they really got mad, but they sure got awfully hot."

The brother's arguments became a necessary part of their process of discovery. While urgently defending a point of view, each brother also listened to and remembered what the other brother said. This give and take, noisy as it sounded to others, was Will and Orv's way of probing a problem from every angle.

Orville said, "After long arguments we often found ourselves in the ludicrous position of each having been converted to the other's side, with no more agreement than when the discussion began."

The 1903 machine was stronger than the previous gliders so it could handle the extra weight and added stress of the engine and other equipment. It also had a longer wingspan—over 40 feet (12 km). For balance, the brothers located the engine on the lower wing to the right of the pilot and built two moveable rudders on the tail. They used two propellers and wings with rigid front edges so only the rear, outer wingtips could be flexed by cable. (This innovation accomplished the same task as **ailerons** on modern planes.)

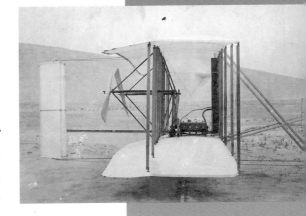

A side view of the 1903 Flyer. Note the machine's vertical rudders.

Despite its size and complexity, the new machine cost the brothers well under $1000 to build. The bicycle business had financed all of their work so far.

HARD LUCK AT KITTY HAWK

A devastating storm raged for days after the Wrights arrived at Kitty Hawk in September 1903. While they repaired damage to a new building and assembled the flying machine, winter began to blow in early. Every morning, Orv and Will had to chip and melt the ice in their washbasin. At night, they huddled under piles of blankets and clothes. Loose **sprockets** and damaged propeller shafts crippled their machine. For replacements, Orville traveled all the way back to Dayton. These troubles cost the brothers five weeks in delays.

The brothers were anxious to test the Flyer before more storms rumbled in, but tough luck persisted. The first time they rolled the Flyer down their new launching track, its tail frames broke. On December 14, a coin toss gave Wilbur first crack at flying, but his test failed due to wind and a poor start. Worse, the front rudder

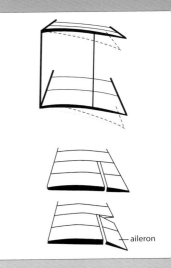

The wing-warping system on the 1903 Flyer (top) allowed the rear edges of the wings to curl. Modern planes (bottom) use ailerons to achieve the same effect as this system.

Langley's Last Try

While returning to Kitty Hawk by train, Orville read a startling newspaper article. On December 8, a pilot had tested Dr. Langley's engine-powered aerodrome for the second time. (The first attempt occurred on October 7.) As had happened with the first test, the aerodrome zoomed off its launching track atop a houseboat on the Potomac River and "simply slid into the water like a handful of mortar."

Wilbur immediately wrote to Octave Chanute. "I see Langley has had his fling. It seems to be our turn to throw now. I wonder what our luck will be."

was damaged. Finally, on December 17, it was Orville's turn to fly.

A DAY FOR THE HISTORY BOOKS

Despite the biting cold, the brothers began the day as always, taking turns washing, shaving, and using the little cook stove. They dressed in their usual white shirts, stiff collars, suits, and ties. "The conditions were very unfavorable as we had a cold, gusty north wind blowing almost a gale," Wilbur explained to Chanute later. "Nevertheless, as we had set our minds on being home by Christmas, we determined to go ahead."

The brothers hoisted a flag to signal the Kill Devil lifesaving station for assistance. They laid down four sections of starting track. Then four members of the lifesaving team and Johnny Moore, a young boy, helped position the machine on the track. Orv and Will walked to the rear of the machine. Simultaneously, each man turned a propeller. The engine coughed, started, and began to warm up.

Orville set up his box camera on a tripod, focusing it on a spot near the end of the starting track. He instructed John T. Daniels, one of the life-

A Kitty Hawk lifesaving team

savers, to snap the camera bulb at the moment the flying machine left the track. Then, as one of the lifesaving crew recalled later, Orville and Wilbur shook hands. "We couldn't help notice how they held on to each other's hand, sort o' like two folks parting who weren't sure they'd ever see one another again." Orville boarded the machine, lying with his hips in the wing-warping cradle. At about 10:35 he pulled a lever and the machine chugged slowly down the track.

With icy wind blowing in his ears, Orville could not hear the men cheering as the Flyer rose a few feet above the sand, engine coughing, propellers whirling.

At exactly the right moment, J.T. Daniels snapped the photograph. It would become one of the most famous photo shots in history.

An historic moment. With Wilbur Wright running alongside, Orville Wright pilots the 1903 Flyer in the world's first powered, controlled flight.

Twelve Seconds to Glory

Of his historic flight, Orv would later recall: "The course of the flight up and down was exceedingly erratic, partly due to the irregularity of the air, and partly to lack of experience in handling this machine . . . As a result the machine would rise suddenly to about ten feet, and then as suddenly dart for the ground. . . . This flight lasted only 12 seconds, but it was nevertheless the first in the history of the world in which a machine carrying a man had raised itself by its own power into the air in full flight, had sailed forward without reduction of speed, and had finally landed at a point as high as that from which it had started."

CHAPTER 5

SAFE AND PRACTICAL

W hen Will and Orv returned home for Christmas, few outside their proud family seemed interested in their world-changing flight. Their press releases mentioned Wilbur's final flight at Kitty Hawk, which lasted a remarkable fifty-nine seconds for a distance of 852 feet (260 km). Following Dr. Langley's dismal flop, however, Americans were not about to fall for more flying hullabaloo. Except for a few misquoted, ridiculously exaggerated reports, the Wrights' news was ignored.

A News Item?

With his brothers' telegram about their historic flights in his hand, Lorin Wright went to the offices of the *Dayton Journal* to find Frank Tunison, the local reporter for the Associated Press. Tunison's response became legendary in newspaper circles. Misquoting the duration of the Wrights' longest flight of the day, he said to Lorin, "Fifty-seven seconds, hey? If it had been fifty-seven minutes, then it might have been a news item."

Orville Wright sent this telegram to his family after he and Wilbur completed the third successful flight of the 1903 Flyer on December 17, 1903.

Will and Orv realized they'd have to show the world a safer and more dependable flying machine if they wanted to market their planes. By New Year's Day, 1904, Orville was already at work with Charlie Taylor building a new and improved engine.

As the Wrights developed a new Flyer, they decided to skip Kitty Hawk that year. Huffman Prairie, a 100-acre (40-hectare) pasture near Dayton, would do for testing. Unlike the soft, sandy shore of Kitty Hawk, the surface of this cow field was bumpy and full of vegetation. Will and Orv cleared the field by hand with scythes. They laid the launching-track rail on the uneven ground and built a portable **derrick**, rigged with ropes and pulleys, to catapult Flyer II along the track. At one corner of the field they also built a wooden shed. The brothers frequently chased cows and horses away from the shed, and soon neighboring farmers were wondering what sort of contraption was taking shape inside it.

Charlie Taylor (third from left) and Wilbur (fourth from left) stand by the launching derrick while timing one of Orville's flights.

Wasting Time

"Wilbur and Orville rode an electric trolley back and forth between Huffman Prairie and Dayton. Luther Beard, a frequent fellow passenger, said, 'I sort of felt sorry for them. They seemed like well-meaning decent young men. Yet there they were, neglecting their business to waste their time day after day on that ridiculous flying machine. I had an idea they must worry their father.'"
Quote from *The Bishop's Boys* by Tom Crouch.

Flyer II was almost a clone of the Wright's 1903 Flyer, which had racked up a total of ninety-eight seconds in the air during its four flights at Kitty Hawk. The brothers hoped for much more from the 1904 machine.

The launching derrick improved lift-offs from the field, but short hops seemed the best Flyer II could do. Its crashes grew more dangerous the higher the brothers made it climb. Orv and Will kept ointments handy to soothe their bruises and scrapes. The owner of Huffman Prairie watched the brothers and said, "They're crazy."

TURNING

Orv and Will practiced banking and turning while testing their constant improvements to Flyer II, and they made slow but steady progress. On September 15, 1904, Wilbur made a turn in the air. Five days later, he flew the first complete circle in the history of the world. Amos Root, the owner of a beekeeping supply house who had just met the Wrights that morning, witnessed the flight. Later, in an article, he wrote, "When it turned that circle, and came near the starting-point, I was right in front of it; and I said then, and I believe still, it was. . . the grandest sight of my life."

On November 9, Wilbur flew four complete circles in five minutes over Huffman Prairie. Accidents, however, happened frequently. Controlling the 1904 flyer was still a problem. It was neither safe nor useful enough.

Soaring over Huffman Prairie in 1905, Orville Wright banks the Flyer to the left.

"WHAT'S GOING ON AT HUFFMAN PRAIRIE?"

In 1905, as the brothers continued to improve both their flying machine and their skill in piloting it, Dayton residents began to take notice. A small crowd gathered at Huffman Prairie on October 5th, when Wilbur set a record for flying time in the Wrights' Flyer III. Circling the field thirty times in thirty-nine minutes, Wilbur covered a distance of 24.5 miles (41 km). Amos Stauffer, who owned a farm bordering the Huffman field, was watching. "The durned thing just kept going round," he said. "I thought that it would never stop."

With this landmark flight, the Wright brothers proved their flying machine could take off, bank and turn, stay in the air for as long as the fuel lasted, and then land safely. After nine

Orville flies high over Huffman Prairie.

The U.S. patent finally granted to the Wright brothers in 1906

More Patent Problems

In 1905, the Wrights still had not received a patent for their flying machine in the United States. Even so, Wilbur offered to sell the U.S. Army a flyer. The Army, however, had received a storm of public criticism for squandering $50,000 on Langley's failed aerodrome, and it was in no mood to spend more for the Wrights' flying machine. For fear of jeopardizing sales elsewhere, the Wrights announced they would no longer test their plane publicly.

England, France, and Great Britain had granted patents to the Wrights in 1904. The brothers decided to look for buyers in those countries.

Denial of a U.S. patent put the Wrights in a dangerous position. People interested in manu-facturing flying machines were eager to make their own use of the Wrights' discoveries, and ideas taken from their hard-gained work could rob the brothers of their future income in aircraft sales. A patent would give the brothers official recognition of their work, as well as provide protection under the law. Interested manufacturers or inven-tors would have to pay the Wrights for use of their patented inventions.

The U.S. government did finally grant the Wrights patent No. 821,393 in May, 1906.

years of study, trial and error, risk-taking, and working through disappointment, the brothers had done it! They had safely flown a practical flying machine for the first time in the history of humankind.

FLYERS OR LIARS?

Three years after the Wright brothers' first flight, most people in the United States and abroad still refused to give them credit for bringing flight to the world. After all, only a handful of people had ever been invited to see a Wright Flyer in action. In 1906, the headline of a Paris newspaper read "Flyers or Liars?" The article summed up doubts on both sides of the Atlantic Ocean. "The Wrights have flown or they have not flown. They possess a machine or they do not possess one. They are in fact either fliers or liars."

Octave Chanute urged the brothers to unveil their machine. Wilbur was considering several offers to buy Wright planes, and each offer required the Flyer to be demonstrated in specific tests. But Orville and Wilbur, perhaps unreasonably, insisted they would not demonstrate their machine until they had signed a contract for a sale. Besides, the Wrights argued, they could afford to be patient. Their efforts were five years ahead of any other experiments with flight.

Wilbur and Orville had made an unwise assumption. In 1906 and 1907, other people—in both the United States and abroad—were already piloting primitive flying machines and trying hard to overtake the Wright brothers' achievements.

THE TRIUMPHANT YEARS

Working out of the public eye for two and a half years, the brothers developed the Wright Type A Flyer, which featured important improvements. It was the first Wright brothers flying machine that allowed a pilot to sit upright, operating the controls like the driver of an automobile. Using two levers, the pilot controlled the tail rudder, wing-warping system, and **elevator**.

By 1908, the Wright brothers had finally made two great sales. They signed a contract promising the U.S. Army Signal Corps they could provide a flying machine "capable of carrying two men and sufficient fuel supplies for a flight of 125 miles [200 km], with a speed of at least 40 miles [63 km] an hour." Shortly after, the brothers signed a contract with a French company. Both contracts would be cancelled if the brothers could not make good on their promises.

RETURN TO KITTY HAWK: 1908

To sharpen their skills with the flight controls of the new Flyer, the brothers returned to Kitty Hawk for the first time in five years. They welcomed a surprise visitor, Charlie Furnas, a Dayton mechanic who longed to fly. After lending a hand setting up camp, Charlie got his wish—and helped the brothers make another historic flight. On May 14, 1908, with Charlie in the passenger seat, the Type A became the first plane to carry two people into the air. Reporters had hidden in the brush to spy on the flight, but they had little success in convincing either their editors or their readers that the Wrights were making history. Most people still were not ready to believe practical flight was possible.

In June, the brothers began the work of fulfilling their contract requirements. Orville returned to Dayton to build and demonstrate a flyer for the Signal Corps, while Wilbur immediately set sail for France, where he prepared for flight demonstrations. The brother's financial future depended on their successes.

Wilbur did not begin flights until early August. At a racecourse near Le Mans, France, he lived in the shed that housed the Flyer, determined to guard his machine from prying eyes. Finally, on August 8, Wilbur circled the racecourse field twice, in four deeply banked turns, and landed. His flight of only two minutes stunned the small crowd of French spectators. Never had they imagined such beautiful control of an airplane.

Wilbur in 1908 with Mrs. Hart Berg, who is about to become the first woman to fly. Her husband tied her skirt with ropes so no one would see her ankles.

Flyers, Not Liars!

After several days of Wright Flyer demonstrations at Le Mans before growing crowds, a reporter for the French newspaper *Le Figaro* wrote, "I've seen him; I've seen them! Yes! I have today seen Wilbur Wright and his great white bird; the beautiful mechanical bird...there is no doubt! Wilbur and Orville Wright have well and truly flown."

Caught in the spotlight at last, Wilbur moved his Flyer to Camp d'Auvours, a larger field belonging to the French Army. The crowd that gathered for his first flight was so large that tickets were issued. Beginning August 21, Wilbur flew day after day at Camp d'Auvours, breaking records and proving that he was the king of the air.

Meanwhile, back in the United States, Orville had arrived at Fort Myer, Virginia, near Washington, D.C., to begin fulfilling the contract requirements for the U.S. Army Signal Corps.

Orville wore his usual neat suit and billed cap to launch his first flight on September 3, 1908. In one minute and eleven seconds, he made a circle and a half above the Fort Myer parade grounds. Not much to brag about, newsmen reported. But each day for the next week and a half, as crowds grew larger, Orville's flights grew more spectacular. He flew every chance he could, making and breaking records almost daily. Engine problems and dangerous winds, however, grounded him for five days.

A FATAL FLIGHT

Lieutenant Thomas E. Selfridge, a member of the U.S. Army's official reviewing team, rode with Orville on his first flight following the delay. Circling three times over the parade ground, Orville kept the Flyer at a low altitude. Then, intending to make a wider turn, he was easing the nose up to fly above 100 feet (30 km) when he heard a slight tapping at the rear of the airplane. The flight then quickly went wrong. As Orville struggled with the controls, the left wing dropped, pulling the nose down. The Flyer was now headed straight for the ground. Moving at top speed when it crashed, the machine flipped over, burying Orville and Selfridge in a tangle of fabric, metal, wood, and dust.

An illustration of the world's first fatal airplane accident on September 17, 1908. Selfridge is depicted falling out, but he was in the plane when it crashed.

Having already freed Orville, rescuers at Fort Myer attempt to remove Selfridge from the wreckage of the 1908 Flyer.

Both men were unconscious and bleeding heavily as stretchers were lifted to carry them away. At the post hospital, doctors found Orville in shock. Although he had suffered several broken bones, an injured back, and scalp wounds, he would survive. Selfridge, with a severely fractured skull, would not.

The accident marked the first death in a Wright flying machine, and the Wright family was devastated. A split in one of the propellers had caused the accident. The U.S. Army allowed the brothers to postpone further demonstration flights at Fort Myer until the summer of 1909.

When a visiting friend asked Orville if he had lost his nerve for flying after the crash, Orville replied, "Oh, you mean will I be afraid to fly again? The only thing I'm afraid of is that I can't get well soon enough to finish those tests next year."

A SLOW RECOVERY

Katharine left her teaching job to stay at Orville's bedside the entire seven weeks he was hospitalized. But even as her brother struggled to recover, Katharine suspected his rivals were attempting to copy his ideas. She was furious when she learned that members of the Aerial Experiment Association had measured the crated remains of the Flyer. Katharine knew a new world race was heating up—to build and sell flying machines.

Returning to Dayton with Kate, Orv healed slowly. For months he walked with a cane, and he never fully recovered from his injuries. Severe back pain hampered him for the rest of his life.

By January 1909, Orv had recovered sufficiently to sail with Kate for France, where they would join Wilbur. Will had been busy. Between August 8, 1908, and January 2, 1909, he had completed 129 flights and established nine world records. Kings, queens, and millionaires were flocking to the flying field to meet him. Dinners were given in his honor, and he collected many awards and honors. Katharine and Orville stepped into this social whirl when they met Wilbur and followed him to Pau, France, where he made sixty-four flights. In Italy, on April 24, a cameraman rode with Wilbur and shot the first motion pictures ever taken from an airplane in flight.

Dayton planned a tremendous June homecoming celebration for Will and Orv. On the morning of June 17th, the Wrights woke up to a deafening sound. "Every factory whistle in Dayton was blowing and every bell ringing," wrote Fred Kelly. "Bands were playing and cannons booming" in honor of the Wrights.

Orville and Katharine sail for France.

THE FLYER PAYS OFF

The celebrations had barely ended when Orville and Wilbur departed for Washington, D.C., to complete demonstration flights for the U.S. Army. Huge crowds gathered as Orville exceeded the army's speed and distance requirements, setting an altitude record of 400 feet

World Celebrities

Europeans declared Katharine, Orville, and Wilbur to be down to earth in spite of the brothers' fame. The Wrights' honesty and sense of humor won over strangers, and many people were eager for details about their lives. Newspapers noted that Wilbur seemed extremely intelligent and knowledgeable about art, literature, and world affairs. His portrait and the Flyer were pictured on souvenir postcards everywhere in France.

Later, when Orv demonstrated the Flyer in Germany, crowds of men, women, and children rushed to touch him. German crown prince Friedrich Wilhelm gave Orville the jeweled stickpin from his tie, saying that the diamond "W" in the center now stood for Wright. The Wright brothers were world celebrities in the bright new century.

Orville (left) and Wilbur (center) talk with King Edward VII of England.

In July 1909, Orville flies over crowds at Fort Myer.

(122 km). The army paid the Wrights $30,000 for their Flyer and Orville began training the first Army pilots.

Not long after the Army demonstration trials ended, Wilbur accepted a $15,000 contract to make exhibition flights for a historic event in New York City. In a brilliant piece of showmanship, Wilbur headed the Flyer straight for the Statue of Liberty. Hundreds of ships that had gathered in the harbor for the celebration tooted and honked as Wilbur banked deeply and circled the Statue of Liberty's waist.

For his second flight, Will traveled 10 miles (16 km) up the Hudson River and back. One million excited spectators witnessed some portion of his exhibition. The public could no longer claim that flying was impossible.

By 1909, two Wright Flyer companies were operating in Europe, but one had not yet been established in the United States. The Wrights took steps to form the Wright Company for manufacturing planes in a Dayton factory. They negotiated an arrangement with investors, agreeing to sell their patent rights and expertise for $100,000 in cash and other benefits. Finally, the brothers' inventions were bringing them more than fame.

Hopes Delayed

The bothers had hoped that the formation of their new company would free them to do the research they loved. But as they continued to invent or redesign parts for the new planes being developed, they were pulled back into the courts. Repeatedly, they were forced to defend their patents against those who they claimed had used their ideas illegally. Wilbur's hopes to return to experiments vanished, and Orville was kept busy training pilots at their new flying school.

TOGETHER FOR THE LAST TIME

On May 25, 1910, the Wrights took rare time out for themselves and went to Huffman Prairie. Two family "firsts" happened that afternoon. With Orville piloting, the brothers flew together for the first and only time. Later, Orville took his father up for his first airplane ride (at the age of eighty-two), with the bishop shouting, "Higher, Orville, higher!

By early 1912, Wilbur's constant attention to legal matters, as well as the brothers' business interests abroad, had kept him constantly on the move and left him exhausted. Wilbur was forty-five years old. While he hoped to retire to research, he was still dealing with lawsuits to protect Wright patents. In late April, while in Boston, Wilbur fell ill. On his return to Dayton on May 2, the Wright family drove to the large spread the brothers had purchased in the suburb of Oakwood. An architect was ready to draw up plans for a house the Wrights would build there. After the trip, Wilbur felt feverish, so the bishop called for Dr. D.B. Conklin. Wilbur's illness was eventually diagnosed as typhoid fever. On the morning of May 30, 1912, he passed away.

In his diary, the bishop noted that his son was forty-five years, one month, and fourteen days old. "A short life, full of consequences," Milton wrote of Wilbur. "An unfailing intellect, imperturbable temper, great self-reliance and as great modesty, seeing the right clearly, pursuing it steadfastly, he lived and died."

New Wright Flyers are assembled at the Wright Company factory in Dayton.

A Glider Scores Again

In October 1911, Orville returned to Kitty Hawk to test an automatic **stabilizer** that he and Wilbur had invented. Lorin and his son, Buster, came along. Orville had built a newly designed glider for the tests. Since newspaper reporters had followed the Wrights, the control device was never tested, but Orville piloted the glider for over fifty flights. During his best flight, Orville hovered, as though suspended in the air, for almost ten minutes. Orville set a new world record for soaring that remained unbroken for ten years.

CHAPTER 7

FORWARD WITHOUT WILL

On Easter Sunday, March 23, 1913, heavy rains fell over a broad area around Dayton, draining in creeks and rivers to the center of the city. Within two days, with levees and a reservoir breaking apart upstream, Dayton was flooded in the worst natural disaster in its history. Luckily, the Wrights' home was safe on higher ground. Orv and Kate's fears focused on the equipment, records, papers, and photographs stored in and behind the bicycle shop.

Although the equipment on the first floor had been destroyed, records and papers on the second floor were relatively undamaged. But the irreplaceable collection of glass plate photography negatives the brothers had shot during their flying machine experiments had been stored in the shed behind the shop. Orville found the negatives in better shape than he had dared to hope. While the emulsion had begun to peel from some of the plates, not one was a total loss. To Orville's great relief, the priceless photo taken by John Daniels of the first flight in 1903 was barely damaged. But Orville's biggest surprise was the discovery of the crated remnants of their 1903 flying machine, protected from the flood under a thick layer of mud.

A photo of Hawthorn Street in Dayton during the flood of 1913. The flood devastated the city of Dayton.

SELLING THE COMPANY

After the flood, when the Wright factory was ready to roll into production again, Orville returned to oversee-

A Tale of Deception

The saga of the Wright brothers' 1903 Flyer—the machine used for their historic first flights—is the sorriest yet most triumphant story of the brothers' quest for recognition. Its subplot of deceit once shamed officials at the Smithsonian Institution, which for many years refused to credit the Wrights for their achievment.

About 1910, the Wright brothers offered the 1903 flying machine to the Smithsonian Institution. But the Smithsonian was run by friends of Dr. Samuel Pierpont Langley, and following Langley's death they rejected the brothers' offer. They were determined to honor Langley as the inventor of the first machine capable of flight, even though his aerodromes had failed.

The Wrights and their supporters objected. In 1914, Smithsonian officials permitted a rival of the Wrights to restore and retest Langley's aerodrome. No impartial officials oversaw the repairs or testing at Hammondsport, N.Y., and the best the machine could manage was a five-second hop. Yet the Smithsonian hung it for display bearing a label that falsely named it "the first man-carrying aeroplane in the history of the world capable of sustained free flight."

In 1915, Orville Wright pointed out obvious changes made to Langley's machine during its restoration, and in 1921 an English aeronautical scientist delivered a report exposing more. Still, the Smithsonian officials would not budge. The Science Museum of London had asked to exhibit the Wright 1903 Flyer. So, in 1928, Orville reluctantly sent it to England.

When Dr. Charles G. Abbot became secretary and director of the Smithsonian Institution in 1928, he inherited this mess. Many associated with the Smithsonian opposed admitting any mistake or fraud. Between 1933 and 1942, Dr. Abbot tried without luck to find a solution. Finally, in 1942, he issued an official statement. "It is everywhere acknowledged that the Wright brothers were the first to make sustained flights in a heavier-than-air machine at Kitty Hawk, North Carolina, on December 17, 1903." The statement went on for pages, confessing that the Smithsonian had not acknowledged thirty-five changes that were made to Langley's original aerodrome to enable its five-second hop at Hammondsport in 1914.

With this official apology, Orville Wright made provisions in his will for the return of the 1903 Flyer to the United States, where it would be exhibited by the Smithsonian Instituion.

ing the company, but his heart was not in it. Struggling with the loss of his brother's partnership—as well as back pain from the 1908 accident—Orville found it hard to make business decisions.

By 1915, Orville was forty-two years old. All of the patent lawsuits had been resolved to his satisfaction, so he sold his interest in the Wright Company and retired from the airplane business.

Winter at Hawthorn Hill, where Orville lived from 1914 until his death in 1948

Orville was happiest tinkering and inventing.

FREE TO TINKER

Orville oversaw the completion of Hawthorn Hill, the Wrights' lavish mansion in Oakwood. At the mansion, he created countless household devices, including a vacuum cleaning system built into the walls and a bathroom water system that encircled the bather from shoulder to knees with shower pipes. Orville generously made the mansion available for many family gatherings.

Finally, Orville was free to build the fine experimental laboratory he and Wilbur had dreamed about when they purchased a lot near the old bicycle shop in 1909. At first, Orville wasn't sure what kind of research he would explore, but his unquenchable thirst for tinkering took over. He repaired clocks, doorbells, and any broken gadget in sight. He made toys for his young relatives and labor-saving inventions for his cabin on a Canadian lake. For many years, he tried to perfect an automatic record changer.

A LIVING LEGEND

By the mid-1920s, Orville had become a living legend, a model for Americans who sought to achieve their own

successes. But Orville had never overcome his shyness. While he took responsibility for representing Wilbur and the Wright family name, he had difficulty accepting public admiration. He absolutely refused to speak in public. During his long-term service on a number of aeronautical boards and commissions, he showed excellent attendance but little leadership

Perhaps, as some have suggested, Orville's continual invention of mechanical gadgets became his shield from the public. When designing, crafting, and repairing, this shy man found a private space.

On December 18, 1928, a ceremony was held for the unveiling of a monument at Kitty Hawk commemorating the Wright brothers' first flight. Orville (in front of the monument) and Amelia Earhart (far right) were among the people who attended.

HONORED AT LAST

On January 30, 1948, Orville Wright died after suffering a heart attack. Eleven months later, the Wrights' 1903 Flyer was installed in its rightful place of honor at the Smithsonian Institution. On the forty-fifth anniversary of the brothers' first flight, the flyer was formally dedicated at the Smithsonian with this inscription:

The Wright brothers ushered in the era of flight, which has been full of many amazing accomplishments.

*THE ORIGINAL WRIGHT BROTHERS' AEROPLANE
THE WORLD'S FIRST
POWER-DRIVEN HEAVIER-THAN-AIR MACHINE IN WHICH MAN
MADE FREE, CONTROLLED, AND SUSTAINED FLIGHT
INVENTED AND BUILT BY WILBUR AND ORVILLE WRIGHT
FLOWN BY THEM AT KITTY HAWK, NORTH CAROLINA
DECEMBER 17, 1903
BY ORIGINAL SCIENTIFIC RESEARCH THE WRIGHT BROTHERS
DISCOVERED THE PRINCIPLES OF HUMAN FLIGHT
AS INVENTORS, BUILDERS, AND FLYERS
THEY FURTHER DEVELOPED THE AEROPLANE, TAUGHT MAN TO
FLY, AND OPENED THE ERA OF AVIATION.*

In 1903, most of the world did not believe humans would ever fly. The Wright brothers remain an inspiration to those dreaming of the impossible.

TIMELINE

1867	Wilbur Wright is born on April 16 near Millville, Indiana
1871	Orville Wright is born on August 19 in Dayton, Ohio
1885	Will is injured in a skating accident at age eighteen; Orv starts a printing business at age fourteen
1889	Will and Orv's mother, Susan Wright, dies on July 4 in Dayton
1892	Orv and Will buy safety bicycles; in December, they open Wright Cycle Shop
1896	Wright brothers begin manufacturing their own line of bicycles
1899	Will and Orv build and fly a biplane kite
1900	Wright brothers fly their first glider at Kitty Hawk, NC
1901	Brothers conduct wind tunnel research with almost two hundred handmade airfoils
1902	Wrights' third glider flies nearly a thousand times, proving the accuracy of their research
1903	Wrights build and fly the world's first powered flying machine that can hold a pilot and be controlled by that pilot
1905	The Wright Flyer III flies 24.5 miles (41 km) in thirty-nine minutes
1906	U.S. government grants Wrights a patent for their flying machine
1908	Wrights sign contracts in the United States and France for the sale of their planes and become world celebrities. A plane crash at Fort Myer results in serious injuries for Orville and the death of Lt. Thomas Selfridge
1909	With flight trials completed, Wrights make first Flyer sales and form Wright Company
1912	Wilbur dies of typhoid fever on May 30
1915	Orville sells the business and retires
1948	Orville dies of a heart attack on January 30

aeronautics: the science of flight, concerning the design, construction, and flying of an aircraft.

ailerons: hinged sections at the rear edge of an airplane's wings that are used to control the rolling of the airplane.

airfoil: an object, such as an airplane wing or propeller, designed to produce a certain force against the flow of air.

apprentice: a person who learns a trade by working for a person or group of people practicing that trade.

biplane: an aircraft with two sets of wings, one above the other.

derrick: a tall, towerlike framework that supports cables and pulleys used for moving objects.

downdraft: a strong downward flow or thrust of wind.

elevator: a hinged airfoil at the rear edge of an airplane's stabilizer that helps control the downward and upward tilting motion of the airplane.

enterprising: being independent and willing to experiment or take risks.

horsepower: a unit of measurement for an engine's power that was originally based on the pulling strength of one horse.

lift: the force supporting an aircraft in flight that results from air moving against the aircraft's wings.

patent: a legal document granting to a person the exclusive right to make, use, and sell a particular invention.

rudder: on an airplane, a hinged, flat piece at the tail that aids in steering.

sprockets: wheels with teeth that fit the links of a chain.

stabilizer: on an airplane, a horizontal airfoil at the tail that helps keep the airplane on a level course.

tuberculosis: a serious disease of the lungs, once infecting millions of people, that causes fever and cough and can be fatal if not treated properly.

typhoid fever: a serious infection, usually caused by drinking contaminated water or milk, that can cause fever and death.

wingspan: the distance from the tip of one wing to the tip of the other wing.

TO FIND OUT MORE

BOOKS

Burleigh, Robert. *Into the Air: The Story of the Wright Brothers' First Flight.* San Diego: Harcourt, Inc., 2002.

Busby, Peter and Craig, David. *First to Fly: How Wilbur and Orville Wright Invented the Airplane.* New York: Crown Publishing Group, 2003.

Collins, Mary and Tunstall, Jo (Ed.). *Airborne: A Photobiography of Orville and Wilbur Wright.* Washington, D.C.: National Geographic Society, 2003.

Freedman, Russell. *The Wright Brothers: How They Invented the Airplane.* New York: Holiday House, 1994.

Jefferis, David. *Aircraft.* New York: DK Publishing, 1997.

Oxlade, Chris. *Flight (Timeliners).* Hauppauge, New York: Barrons Educational Series, Inc., 2001.

Sullivan, George. *The Wright Brothers (In Their Own Words).* New York: Scholastic, 2003.

INTERNET SITES

Wright Brothers Aeroplane Company & Museum of Pioneer Aviation
www.first-to-fly.com
A virtual museum of pioneer flight.

The Wright Experience
www.wrightexperience.com
Research and documentation for authentic reproductions of Wright aircraft.

The Wright Brothers: Pioneers in Aviation
www.si.edu/archives/documents/ wright.htm
Smithsonian Institution web site discussing the Wright Brothers.

The Franklin Institute Online: The Wright Brothers
www.fi.edu/wright
Film footage, historical artifacts, and educational articles about the Wright brothers.

Kitty Hawk—Kill Devil Hills
www.outerbanks.com/wrightbrothers/ wrightlc.htm
Wright brothers' Kitty Hawk photographs, from 1900 to 1911.

About the Author

Gretchen Will Mayo was born in Dayton, Ohio, as were her parents, grandparents, and great-grandparents. Her mother's family lived close to Hawthorn Hill and knew associates of the Wrights. Dr. Conklin was the doctor for her mother's family, and Dr. Theodore Lily, her mother's close friend, was Orville Wright's dentist for over twenty years. Ms. Mayo lives in Wisconsin with her husband, Tom. They have three adult daughters. Ms. Mayo has published many books for children, and she is also a teacher and illustrator. She has a Masters in Fine Arts in Writing for Children from Vermont College.